WISDOM FROM GOD

MEDITATIONS FROM CAROLYN

(Journeys through Life)

CAROLYN L. REYNOLDS

Copyright © 2007 by Carolyn L. Reynolds

Wisdom From God – Meditations From Carolyn
by Carolyn L. Reynolds

Printed in the United States of America

ISBN 978-1-60034-840-2
IBSN 1-60034-840-8

All rights reserved solely by the author. The author guarantees all contents are original and do not infringe upon the legal rights of any other person or work. No part of this book may be reproduced in any form without the permission of the author. The views expressed in this book are not necessarily those of the publisher.

Unless otherwise indicated, Bible quotations are taken from King James Version. Copyright © 1988 by Author.

www.xulonpress.com

CONTENTS

Introduction vii

Enlightenment-Repentance
Romans 2:11 13

Love Your Enemies
Luke 6:35 21

Jennifer
Psalm 37:3-5 27

A Conversation with Jennifer
James 4:2c…1 John 3:22 33

Wisdom from Heaven
James 3:13-18 41

Robin and My Father
2 Peter 3:9 49

Dream – May 1992
Proverbs 4:1 59

A Specific Word
Isaiah 54:2, 3 63

Prayer Partners
Galatians 6:2 79

Prayer for Salvation 87

INTRODUCTION

I have kept a spiritual diary, or you may call it a prayer journal, for many years. I record in it, my personal and private talks with God, my supplications, my thanks, incidents, situations and events in my life that God has brought me through.

I record unction's and leadings by the Holy Ghost; also dreams and visions. When I don't understand what is happening in my life, or why some particular person has come into my life for a seemingly significant purpose, I record my questions to the Holy Ghost. I also record the answers that I receive.

What I have recorded in my prayer journals is not as detailed as I am sharing with you in the following encounters. As I read through my journals, the Holy Ghost brought back to my memory the details of what had happened.

I have changed all names except mine, and some genders have been changed, for obvious reasons.

Even though these were circumstances in my life, I attempted to describe them so that if you have, or if you will in the future encounter anything similar, for a start you can gleam from my encounters, to hear from God for yourself.

As God gave me my Scriptures, He will give you your Scriptures. As God gave me my songs, He will give you your songs. As God gave me my mentors, my teachers, my friends, my prayer partners, He will give you your mentors, your teachers, your friends, your prayer partners. Whoever God brings into your life, remember that all the glory, all the honor, all the praise, all the thanks belongs to Him.

I pray that the episodes and scenarios that I am sharing with you from my prayer journal will help you on your spiritual journey. I hope that you will be encouraged to reach your full potential in God. My desire in sharing some of my personal prayer journal entries with you is to realize what have exploded in my life. That is the absolute truth of;

Deuteronomy 8:3b...
That he might make thee know that man doth not live by bread only, but by every word that proceedeth out of the mouth of the LORD doth man live.

Matthew 4:4...
But he answered and said, It is written, Man shall not live by bread alone, but by every word that proceedeth out of the mouth of God.

God, in eternity, still speaks to us today, out of eternity, with wisdom, power and compassion. God speaks to us in visions and dreams, in life's lessons, and in other people, today.

Joel 2:28,29...
And it shall come to pass afterward, that I will pour out my spirit upon all flesh; and your sons and your daughters shall prophesy, your old men shall dream dreams, your young men shall see visions:

Acts 2:17,18...
And it shall come to pass in the last days, Saith God, I will pour out of my Spirit upon all flesh: and your sons and your daughters shall prophesy, and your young men shall see visions, and your old men shall dream dreams: And on my servants and on my handmaidens I will pour out in those days of my Spirit; and they shall prophesy:

The Holy Spirit tells us daily what we need to know in every situation we face, and in every circumstance we encounter. In the Bible there are recorded absolute truths that we must adhere to; and there are principles and practices (ways of accomplishing directives) that we must follow. We cannot in spoken language, or in the written word define the dimension of eternity.

Hebrews 1:1,2...
GOD, who at sundry times and in divers manners Spake in time past unto the fathers by the prophets, Hath in these last days spoken unto us by his Son, whom he hath appointed heir of all things, by whom also he made the worlds;

John 14:26
But the Comforter, which is the Holy Ghost, whom the Father will send in my name, he shall teach you all things, and bring all things to your remembrance, whatsoever I have said unto you.

God commands us many times in the Bible; 'He that hath an ear, let him hear.'
(*Romans 10:14*, and *Titus 1:3* tells us that His word was manifested through preaching, 'speaking and hearing'. I also want to encourage you to read the Bible out loud.)
The Bible tells us in;

Psalm 119:89...
For ever, O LORD, thy word is settled in heaven.

All that has been settled in heaven can not be captured with pen and pencil on paper. What does God want us to hear? He wants us to hear what He has settled in heaven, and obey His Word. He wants us to hear what He is saying NOW. How do we hear God? We learn to hear Him by reading His Word recorded in the Bible. In His written Word are absolutes; and there are written principles and practices that we are to follow as we are led by His Holy Spirit. The Bible is a guide on how to hear Him, and how to understand and obey what we hear, not so much with our natural ear, but with our spiritual (inner) ear. He wants us to hear what He is saying NOW. He wants us to be led by the Holy Spirit, in every step that we take, in every move that we make, in every word that we speak, and in every thought that we think. Every decision we make should be based on God's Logos Word in the Bible; and by the leading of the Holy Ghost, with confidence that God watches over His Word to perform it (***Jeremiah 1:12***). He has left many details on the rewards of obedience, and on the consequences of disobedience.

Even as you are reading this He is speaking to you about an event that you must resolve, or one that may be in the making for you to encounter. Not one of us is capable of handling anything without the directing of the Holy Spirit. Every adverse encounter must be resolved in a swift and godly manner.

As I read the Bible and attempt to apply the absolute truths of His Word to my life; and when I attempt to apply the principles and practices of His Word in my life, I sometimes need someone in this physical dimension to assist me to take step one, step two, step three. I thank God when He sends someone to help me, someone to hold my hand. When and if you need someone to assist you, God will usher that person into your life.

I fail not to read His Word, listen for His leadings, and obey His directions. I am just like you, human, humble and frail, and I depend on one person and that person only, the Holy Ghost; God speaking to me, Jesus walking with me by my side, and Holy Spirit leading me every step of the way.

The few occasions that I share with you on how I heard the leading of the Lord and how I entered into His Spirit of obedience, may help you or someone you know to do the same. Yes, I've made mistakes. However, our God is loving and forgiving.

We may lose some people in our lives. Not because of death but by association. There are some stands that we must take for the Kingdom of God, and there are ways and desires that our Father wish to manifest on earth, NOW; things that He has already established and settled in eternity.

In conclusion;

In no way do I wish to convey to you that I am a perfect person with a flawless personality, and with desirable characteristics; or that I am always right in all situations. In the scenarios that I am sharing with you, I can only relate to you from my perspective. I don't know, and you won't know why people act and/or react to us the way that they do. Obviously there was something that clashed in our receiving and/or accepting of one another. I am not pointing a finger or trying to find someone to blame for mishaps in my life. We must learn how to act and react to all encounters in our lives. However, only in our response to encounters will we know if we have a heart for God. Our actions are planned. Our reactions come from our very being, from what we have in our hearts.

Proverbs 4:23...
Keep thy heart with all diligence; for out of it are the issues of life.

Matthew12:34b...
For out of the abundance of the heart the mouth speaketh.

When God takes us from glory to glory, that becomes a time of refining (***Zachariah 13:9***), and situations will come to purge the impurities out of us and what is left should shine like gold. Our actions and our reactions should reflect the image of Jesus Christ.

There is nothing in life more precious than us surrendering to God. We are no good to ourselves or anyone else until we receive Jesus Christ as our personal Lord and Savior. I urge you to take the time right now to confess that Jesus is the Son of God, and invite Him into your heart.

ENLIGHTENMENT-REPENTANCE
(ROMANS 2:11)

ROMANS 2:11
FOR THERE IS NO RESPECT OF PERSONS WITH GOD.

LIFE'S LESSONS

It was in the fall or winter of 1972, during a time of building my relationship with God, and building a solid foundation into the kingdom of God, that revelation and enlightenment from Him smacked me right in the face. It was in a Sunday morning worship service that the Holy Ghost began to teach me about unforgiveness and bitterness. I didn't know at the time that unforgiveness and bitterness had taken root in my heart, but it became very clear to me that it had. During that time was when I learned that God is no respecter of persons (and I didn't even know what that meant).

On this particular Sunday morning, after song service, and after the pastor was well into his sermon, a man entered into the sanctuary and sat in the middle of the middle section of the pews.

This man was noticeably drunk, smelling bad and loud, as he made his way pass members of the congregation to sit down. As he rested himself and got comfortable and warm, his head fell back and he went to sleep. He went so sound asleep that he began to snore – loudly. The deacons that sit on the front pew got up to go back (I'm sure to wake him up and usher him out of the church) to where he was sleeping.

WISDOM FROM GOD

As they started on their mission, the pastor stopped preaching and told the deacons not to disturb the man. He said we don't know what led this man to this church (in this area there were churches on every corner) on this Sunday morning and we had better let God handle this situation. He also said that because of this man's apparent state of being, compared to our pious and apparent soberness, it didn't mean that God loved that man any less than us; or that God loved us more than he loved that man. Although his physical body was asleep, his spirit was wide awake, and for whatever reason he was here let his spirit be fed. It was a strong reminder of God's love for all of his creations.

MORE LIFE'S LESSONS

I had recently filed for divorce from my husband of eighteen years. We had four wonderful daughters. Our marriage had been going down hill for a long time. My husband had become more physically abusive (I wasn't a battered wife, however, we had many fights) to me, so I left him. He was what you would call a 'street man', a good provider when it comes to finances. I had recently turned my life over to Jesus, and even though there wasn't a lack of money the arguments were escalating to a point where I was frightened for my life. I knew one of us would eventually get hurt, bad.

I had begun to think that because I now had turned my life over to Jesus, that Jesus loved me more than He loved my husband.

I was a new convert and still a babe in Christ and needed to be taught much. I knew about the love of God, but I didn't know about the extent or magnitude of His **UNCONDITIONAL** love that He has for **all** of His creations. During this particular season of my life I was so emotionally hurt, I felt that because I surrendered to Jesus and served Him, tithed (tithing was the first discipline I learned) that I had more favor with God than my husband. I was so sure that my husband would be punished for hurting me that I would pay close attention to the news media to see when he was going to get his payback. I didn't wish for any thing bad to happen, but in my mind something bad would happen to him.

MORE WISDOM FROM GOD

Wisdom from God told me that as much as I thought that God loves me, He loves my husband to that same degree. (*Acts 10:34*)

MEDITATING ON GOD'S WORD

That day, that Sunday morning worship service, my spirit was quickened inside of me; not only had a revelation of the truth of God's Word, but also that he **UNCONDITIONALLY** loved my husband. I also got a picture of how prideful, haughty and lifted up I was. It wasn't a pretty picture. Right then and there when the pastor said 'God loves that man as much as He loves us', I was convicted by the Holy Spirit of my proud heart. I repented to God before the sermon was over and before the altar call. I didn't go forward to the altar, but the cleansing tears fell full force. I turned around and kneeled at the pew where I was sitting and asked God to forgive me and remove the contempt that I had harbored toward my husband. I asked Him to remove the contempt and replace it with love. I asked Jesus to teach me how to forgive and how to love. My repenting didn't mean that I would drop my divorce proceedings and reunite with my husband, but it did mean that I would be set free from the guilt and bondage of the sin of pride and unforgiveness. It meant that strongholds would be torn down and healing could begin to take place. A cleansing took place and as the love of God engulfed me, I felt the oil of restoration and forgiveness from the hand of Precious Jesus. The Bible says...

1 John 1:9...
If we confess our sins, he is faithful and just to forgive us our sins, and to cleanse us from all unrighteousness.

I experienced the grace and the mercy of God. As the healing process began, joy and strength rose up inside of me.

Nehemiah 8:10b says 'for the joy of the LORD is your strength'.

THANKS TO GOD

I thank God for hearing my prayer of repentance. My repentance was more than saying 'I'm sorry' or 'I didn't mean it'. It meant that I lay aside myself, stop feeling sorry for myself and lay before God with a godly sorrow for my thoughts and actions. As I lay before God, I had to verbally say out loud 'Father, forgive me'. By speaking *1 John 1:9* out loud and repenting out loud, I was releasing anger, malice, hatred and pride; all those strongholds that was keeping me in bondage to the enemy. By speaking out loud the power of God's Word was being released into enemy territory and breaking down hindering barriers and pulling down strongholds.

I, more importantly had to receive the forgiveness that Jesus paid for on the cross; and that He offered me. I had to verbally say 'Jesus I receive your forgiveness, your healing and your reconciling me back to you. Sometimes we as believers conclude that thinking thoughts is all that we need to do, but Jesus said...

John 6:63...
It is the spirit that quickeneth; the flesh profiteth nothing: the words that I speak unto you, they are spirit, and they are life.

God's Words are life and they are to be spoken. We must speak (be audible), to verbalize His Words.

FORGIVENESS

1 John 1:9...
if we confess our sins, he is faithful and just to forgive us our sins, and to cleanse us from all unrighteousness.

In this verse to 'confess' means to speak; express by sound; utter audibly. It means that we are to acknowledge to God what and/or how we have acted, lived, spoken or thought anything contrary to God's Word. It isn't enough to be sorrowful and say 'I'm sorry', 'I didn't mean to do that', or 'I couldn't help myself' or 'the devil made me do it'. We must repent (regret deeply something said or done) and turn away from doing that thing again. When we turn 'away' from doing what is wrong, we must turn 'to' what is right. We must turn 'to' Jesus. Then we are to confess our sins to Jesus and ask him to forgive us. (If possible ask the person or persons that we sinned against to forgive us (***James 5:16***).

We are not held accountable if others don't accept/receive our apologies. It should be audible and sincere. I'm not saying it has to be a public confession. You can go into your prayer closet to speak out to Jesus. Remember, Jesus knows our hearts. He knows if our confession is a godly sorrow. The Bible says that we are to confess our sins. The book of *1 John* is a wonderful study on how to live life in the manner of forgiveness.

From time to time, well meaning people tell us that we must learn to forgive ourselves when it seems that we can't get past an unfortunate event in our lives. **We cannot forgive ourselves.**

Mark 2:7, 10; Luke 5:21, and *Ephesians 4:32* all tell us that only God can forgive man his sins. If we could forgive ourselves, then the man in *Mark 2:3-5,* that was sick of palsy, could have forgiven himself, and his friends wouldn't have had the need to search for Jesus to heal him. If we could forgive ourselves, the sinner woman in *Luke 7:44-48* would have stayed home and said 'I forgive myself'. If we had the power or the ability to forgive ourselves, then it wouldn't have been necessary for Jesus to go to the cross and shed His blood for us. Whether our sins are against God (all sin is really against God), ourselves or against others, we must ask for forgiveness. *Matthew 5:23-25* is a passage of Scripture that we should all practice.

We cannot forgive ourselves.

I have found no Scripture that tell us we are to forgive ourselves. (If I am in error, may the Holy Spirit bring it to my remembrance). *Matthew 6:14, 15; Mark 11:25,* and *Luke 6:37,* tell us that in order for us to be forgiven, we must first forgive men and their trespasses against us. When we forgive others, then we will be in a position to receive forgiveness, and to be restored to a right relationship with God. Unforgiveness opens a door for strongholds to come into our lives and those strongholds block our blessings and distort our view with God. We must confess our sins and petition Jesus to forgive us. (Some more could be said about that previous statement, but not at this time). I have heard it said that unforgiveness could cause physical afflictions. We must be positionally ready to receive forgiveness, like we must be positionally ready to receive blessings. God's love is unconditional, His promises are conditional. We should prepare ourselves to receive, by faith, the finished work of Jesus Christ on his cross (*Colossians 2:14*). It was the blood of Jesus Christ of Nazareth that was shed for our sins. It is His blood alone that can wash away our sins and grant us forgiveness.

1 John 1:7b says...
and the blood of Jesus Christ his Son cleanseth us from all sin.

Colossians 1:14 ...
In whom we have redemption through his blood, even the forgiveness of sins.

Our desires should be to have a broken, humble and contrite (penitent-regretful) heart. A heart that God can shape and mold. If we could forgive ourselves, just think how easy it would be to forgive our deeds and never repent. Then we would be eternally lost.

If you believe that the Bible is the infallible Word of God (and I hope that you do), you will believe that Jesus will forgive you. You will also believe that God has provided a way for you and me to be restored and brought back into a proper relationship with Him. His Word says that he is faithful and just to forgive us our sins.

Thank God for His Perfect Sacrifice, His Son Jesus Christ. Because of God's love for us, and Jesus' willingness to lay down his life, we are saved from eternal damnation.

John 3:16...
For God so loved the world, that he gave his only begotten Son, that whosoever believeth in him should not perish, but have everlasting (eternal) LIFE.

To be cleansed by Jesus is to be purified from the pollution and guilt of sin; and to be redeemed from the penalty of sin. The enemy will attempt to place into our minds the thought that we are guilty and filthy and unclean. However, when we receive by faith, when we accept by faith, when we embrace by faith, the forgiveness that only Jesus Christ can give, we can tell the devil to 'get thee hence behind me. I am covered with the blood of Jesus'.

HALLELUJAH! HALLELUJAH! HALLELUJAH!

ROMANS 2:11

LOVE YOUR ENEMIES
(LUKE 6:35)

LUKE 6:35
BUT LOVE YE YOUR ENEMIES, AND DO GOOD, AND LEND, HOPING FOR NOTHING AGAIN; AND YOUR REWARD SHALL BE GREAT, AND YE SHALL BE THE CHILDREN OF THE HIGHEST: FOR HE IS KIND UNTO THE UNTHANKFUL AND TO THE EVIL.

LIFE'S LESSONS

I had been employed with a worldwide financial corporation for fourteen years, and at the age of forty seven I was promoted to the position of bookkeeper. To accept the promotion I had to move to a city two hundred and fifty two miles from where I was born and raised, where I had married and raised my family. I accepted the challenge.

In this new position I was trained for the duties of accounting supervisor, not bookkeeper. I didn't have the title or salary of supervisor, but I was told by the exiting bookkeeper that these were the duties that I was to perform. Since I was new to this local office I did as I was instructed. Who am I to argue if this position had been handled for the past five years as supervisor? When the exiting bookkeeper moved out of the city to her promotion, I was told by my immediate supervisor that I would no longer be performing the duties that I had been trained. The problem was why I was trained to do a job that I would not be performing?

The accounting procedures were different due to the laws of this state. Working in a position of such responsibility and not being familiar with this state's regulations and guidelines, my performance wasn't what it should have been. I was in quite a dilemma and being a salaried employee (no labor union) I had begun to accumulate verbal and written reprimands, and unfavorable performance gradings. There had been an adverse file compiled against me. This file would hinder me from receiving future promotions, raises and bonuses.

In order to get some balance in my work situation, I requested a conference with my manager, and a third party (a mediator) from the home office. A person that I had hoped would be objective and would intervene for the purpose of producing agreeable working relationship/atmosphere.

While I was waiting for a reply from the home office, the home office had contacted my branch manager. I probably will never know what transpired in that contact. I was called into my branch manager's office after lunch on a Monday afternoon, with him and my immediate supervisor, and for about four hours was severely reprimanded for taking the route that I had taken.

Many of you reading about this episode in my life have experienced the same in your lives. We all have a story of injustice to tell. I am sharing this because others may go through the same situation or similar circumstances.

I didn't know that I was capable of such anger and outrage. I was so angry. In attempting to defend myself from their (branch manager and immediate supervisor) accusations of not being qualified for this position, and with my anger to the boiling point, I didn't have the presence of mind to just open the door and walk out. When I did leave the office I was so tired I felt absolutely exhausted. I was too furious to even cry. I was at a time in my life that I felt I couldn't quit my job. I didn't want to quit my job. I really loved what I was doing.

I had some hard questions to ask myself. If I am to continue working with this corporation, in this present location, and in this same position, how am I to accomplish that? How am I to perform the duties expected of me without more training, giving the same performance that had lead me to this promotion? How am I to lead employees and supervise departments with the animosity that I now felt for this manager and supervisor (which translated 'The Company') and expect to be promoted, receive raises or bonuses? How could I say that I love GOD and feel this hatred toward my employers? I knew that I couldn't live from day to day with hatred and bitterness taking root in my heart, and yet expect God to bless me. I also know that according to **Psalm 66:18** and **Isaiah 59:2**, God cannot bless an unforgiving heart. I asked the Lord, what should I do? How do I handle this situation?

GOD'S WISDOM

God told me to pray for him. (my branch manager more than my immediate supervisor was the biggest instigator of the matter). I said I don't know how to pray for him. There was a silence. God had spoken. Pray for him.

AS I MEDITATED ON GOD'S WORD

I had started a walking exercise program when I moved to this town. In the evening after work I would walk five miles, three days a week. I used these times to pray for my manager. It was during these times that God revealed to me the real meaning of **Luke 6:35**, and all of its connecting Scriptures (some are listed below). That evening when I started my walking exercise, I began with these words;

'Heavenly Father, I come to you in the name of Jesus. I come to you with nothing but love for you, and with obedience unto your command. Forgive me for all transgressions that I have committed and for anything in my life that is displeasing to you. Lord it is hard for me to pray for someone that I have no love in my heart for them. I believe your Word that says...

Proverbs 3:5, 6...
Trust in the LORD with all thine heart; and lean not unto thine own understanding. In all thy ways acknowledge him, and he shall direct thy paths.

And as I begin to pray for my manager I won't come to you pretending that love is in my heart for him because you know my heart and you know what is in it. Lord, I believe you can change my heart. I believe you can change that extreme dislike that I feel and replace it with love. Jesus, only you can change this heart. Your Word says...

Luke 6:27, 28...
But I say unto you which hear, Love your enemies, do good to them which hate you, Bless them that curse you, and pray for them which despitefully use you.

Matthew 5:11, 12...
Blessed are ye, when men shall revile you, and persecute you, and shall say all manner of evil against you falsely, for my sake. Rejoice, and be exceeding glad: for great is your reward in heaven: for so persecuted they the prophets which were before you.

Romans 12:14...
Bless them which persecute you: bless, and curse not.

(I carried my pocket New Testament with me and had marked these Scriptures). Your Word says my reward will be great in heaven. Your love Lord is my reward. I thank you in advance for changing my heart, my personal life, my work life, and all that you touch in answer to this prayer.'

I could walk the five miles in one hour and thirty seven minutes. The next three months I prayed for my manager, his wife, his son, his daughter, his home, his mother, his father, his siblings (if he had any), his pets (if he had any), and the position he held at the corporation. I prayed good, not evil. I prayed blessings, not curses. I prayed love, not hate.

I'm not sure how long into this season of prayer it was that someone asked me if my manager and I had made a truce between us. I asked why did they think that? They said because the two of you seem to have a genuine friendly affection for one another. I hadn't noticed until it was brought to my attention that God had changed my heart. We had been saying 'good morning' and 'goodnight', 'have a good day or weekend' to each other. He had started asking me if I needed help with my work load. There were many pleasantries between us that the entire personnel had noticed. They talked about the workable atmosphere that prevailed.

To God be the glory. God had ushered His grace into my life and changed my heart. I realized that I did have a godly love for this man and his family.

About four months after the argument/disagreement between us, there was an announcement in an office meeting. My manager had been offered a promotion with specific terms, and he had accepted the promotion and agreed to the conditional terms. The offer was to accept a branch manager's position for a three year period in New Zealand. The corporation would pay all of his moving expenses, all travel expenses for him and his family up front. The corporation would purchase the house of his choice (I'm sure there were some guidelines). For the three years he would just pay rental rates. That way if he decided to return to the United States after the three year period, selling a house would not be a concern for him. All company travel between the United States and New Zealand would be paid in advance by the corporation. He wouldn't have to pay expenses out of his pocket and then submit an expense report for reimbursement. He would be compensated financially one time each year for vacation travel expenses for him and his family between the two countries.

What a blessing from God. What an education for his children, and what an opportunity for him and his family to see part of the world free. I thank you Lord that you are no respecter of persons.

As a result of my manager's generous remarks for me on my performance record, I received a bonus (the branch secretary said that it was the largest recorded in that local branch), and a substantial raise in my salary.

THANKS TO GOD

Father, I give you thanks, and I give you praise. Lord Jesus, I am so thankful and grateful that you are no respecter of persons ***Romans 2:11***.

I am so thankful that you love all your creatures the same. I give you thanks for watching over your Word to perform it ***Jeremiah 1:12***. Our rewards are great on this earth and in this life, just as you promise they will be in heaven. Thank you for exceeding my expectations in answered prayer. Thank you for loving me, and for providing for me. Our rewards can't be measured in earthly terms, because you are our Heavenly Father.

LUKE 6:35

JENNIFER
(PSALM 37:3-5)

PSALM 37:3-5...
'TRUST IN THE LORD, AND DO GOOD; SO SHALT THOU DWELL IN THE LAND, AND VERILY THOU SHALT BE FED. DELIGHT THYSELF ALSO IN THE LORD; AND HE SHALL GIVE THEE THE DESIRES OF THINE HEART. COMMIT THY WAY UNTO THE LORD; TRUST ALSO IN HIM; AND HE SHALL BRING IT TO PASS.'

LIFE'S LESSONS

It had been a few months since my retirement, and the Holy Spirit had been dealing with me on the importance of fellowshipping with the saints of God.

A few months before I retired the Lord had ministered to me about the biblical principles of giving offerings. He had taken this knowledge to a new level and to a higher dimension in Him. I received a revelation from God on how to apply the principles and practices recorded in the Bible on sowing financial seed into fertile ground; and how to move myself into a position to receive my harvest.

In this season of my life I began to put into practice what God had taught me about sowing seed into his kingdom. Using that knowledge I made a pledge to support two teaching ministries by sowing financial offerings (seed) to them on a monthly basis.

With these enlightenments (fellowship and sowing) coming to life inside of me, and becoming a reality with me, I began to invite families into my home after Sunday morning worship for dinner and a time of fellowship. I invited entire families, parents, grandparents, children, cousins, aunts and uncles, entire clans. I tried to limit it to three families each week so that we would be comfortable and not feel crowded. We would eat, then visit, sharing testimonies about God working in our lives, and sometimes watch videos that taught on worshiping God with our finances, our time and our substance.

One month later after I made my covenant with God to support two teaching ministries, my pastor (not where I attend now) asked ten members of our congregation to pledge one hundred dollars a month, for twelve months to our church building fund. He didn't ask anyone specific, he wanted the members to volunteer. His reasoning was that if we volunteered, we would be led by God and it would come from our hearts. I wanted to be one of the ten members to pledge, but I had just begun to honor my commitment to God to support the two teaching ministries, so I didn't volunteer to participate in the church pledge drive.

One Sunday after morning worship, Jennifer, a close and personal friend to my family, that also loves the Lord, had joined us for dinner. She wasn't a member of our congregation, so she didn't know about our pastor's request for pledges to the building fund. During our conversation, the subject of the pledge came up and I shared that as much as I wanted to be a part of the drive, I couldn't because of my recent monthly commitments. I said that the only way I would be able to add my name to the list is that God would show me.

I noticed that as we talked about the pledge drive, Jennifer had begun to be restless, and then she left very quickly. I didn't question what seemed to be an abrupt exit, I attributed it to maybe she wasn't feeling well or maybe she had a previous appointment. Jennifer loves to fellowship and share about the goodness of the Lord and what God was doing in her life, and in her families' lives, and she normally would have stayed for the entire evening.

Later that same Sunday, after everyone had gone home, Jennifer called me on the telephone and said that she wanted to come over and talk with me. I said ok, everyone's gone and we could have some privacy, and within one-half hour she was back at my house. She said she left in a hurry earlier that day because when I shared that I wasn't able to participate in the pledge program, the Holy Spirit quickened within her and she had become uncomfortable and had to leave. This is what she shared with me:

'The Holy Spirit instructed me about a month ago for me to give you one hundred dollars a month for ten months. He didn't say why, but I wasn't sure at that time that it was the Holy Spirit. Within myself I didn't understand why I should do this because it didn't appear that you needed the assistance. Now I know that it truly was the Holy Spirit and here I am to tell you that I will begin to give you the dollar amount that I was instructed beginning next month (May 1993). The Holy Spirit told me ten months, but you said your pastor asked for a pledge of twelve months, so I will make it twelve months'.

When we finished thanking God, singing and giving glory and honor to Jesus, praising that Name which is above every Name, the Name of Jesus, I told her to obey GOD rather than man. Make her gift for ten months only as she was instructed, God will provide for the other two months. The next Sunday I added my name to the pledge list.

WISDOM FROM GOD

In my private and quiet time with God, I told him that If Jennifer wasn't able to keep her commitment at any time during the ten month period, that I would help her. I knew that she was recently divorced, that she wasn't working and she had two small children. She was receiving child support and alimony, but I also know the financial hardships a single parent faces. I was impressed by the Holy Spirit not to help her, to allow her to do this herself because it was her charge. (I didn't share with Jennifer, this conversation with God).

OBEYING GOD'S WORD

Jennifer began giving her gift when she said she would. She didn't miss one month during the ten months. Each month she faithfully put into my hands one hundred dollars in an envelope. If I happen not to be at home, she would put it through the mail slot that is in my front door. Each month I faithfully gave that same one hundred dollars to my church to fulfill my pledge commitment. The last two months of Jennifer's commitment to God, I had temporally moved out of town (to care for my father). Jennifer sent the money to me by mail and I sent the pledge to my church by return mail. God provided abundantly for me to pay the eleventh and twelfth months of the pledge.

From the time Jennifer started depositing into my hand her pledge, we never mentioned verbally our agreement with God. It was almost like it was too sacred to speak. We were close friends and communicated almost every day. She and I both knew that this was a special commitment between God and the two of us. It was a sacred bond. Jennifer never questioned me about the seed she faithfully turned over to me each month. She trusted that I would do as God had directed me; and we both had faith in God for our harvest. Neither one of us knew exactly how our harvest would come. I didn't think about it consciously, and I'm certain that she didn't either. She was busy going to school (working on her master's degree), and I was busy caring for my father. I guess in our spirits we knew that God would bless us, and He did. The Bible says...

Proverbs 3:5, 6...
Trust in the Lord with all thine heart; and lean not unto thine own understanding. In all thy ways acknowledge him, and he shall direct thy paths.

Jennifer or I couldn't comprehend in our natural minds what God was about to do in our lives. I thank God for Jennifer and her obedience to Him. He knew of her love for Him and He knew of her willingness to be obedient. Because of God's grace and His abundant blessings, we were instruments, vessels if you will, to testify of the goodness of God.

(This pledge started in May of 1993; my temporary move to care for my father was January 1994; my father went home to be with the Lord September 1995).

THANKS TO GOD

It had been six months since my father passed, and in one of my periods of meditation, the Holy Spirit told me that Jennifer's harvest from her seed planting into me and the church pledge drive was the doors that were opened to assist her in her endeavor to earn her master's degree in Social Work at Michigan State University. Because she truly believed it was God's plan to plant seed into the kingdom of God, and she obeyed the quickening of her spirit, doors that had been shut to her would now be opened, and people would be ushered into her life to help her through the doors and over the hurdles.

We believed Gods' Word. We trusted Him to perform His Word.

Jeremiah 1:12...
Then said the LORD unto me, Thou hast well seen: for I will hasten my word to perform it.

The desires of Jennifer's heart manifested in her life, in her season. Her desire was to be a Social worker. After high school she went to a community college and earned an associate degree. A few years later she went back to college and earned her bachelors degree in Criminal Justice. She then went to work for a worldwide financial corporation. She married, had two children, got divorced, and still had a strong desire to be able to provide counseling services to those in need. The marriage and divorce happened over a period of six years. When the Holy Spirit told me to tell her what her harvest was, and that it was a consequence of, a reward of her obedience to the principle of sowing, I told her and this is her testimony, (printed by permission).

PSALM 37:3-5

A CONVERSION WITH JENNIFER
(JAMES 4:2c...1 JOHN 3:22)

JAMES 4:2c...
'YE FIGHT AND WAR, YET YE HAVE NOT, BECAUSE YE ASK NOT.'

1 JOHN 3:22...
'AND WHATSOEVER WE ASK, WE RECEIVE OF HIM, BECAUSE WE KEEP HIS COMMANDMENTS, AND DO THOSE THINGS THAT ARE PLEASING IN HIS SIGHT.'

Jennifer is a faithful tither, and a generous giver of offerings. God's promise to tither's is

Malachi 3:10...
If I will not open you the windows of heaven, and pour you out a blessing, that there shall not be room enough to receive it.

That translate, that God will present before the tither, windows (more than one), floodgates *Genesis 7:11* doors

Psalm 78:23, of opportunities to advance the kingdom of God. When we are faithful to God's commands, ***Leviticus 26:3-5***, and when we pursue and seize those windows of opportunities, God will heap upon us blessings. When we endeavor to be good stewards over what He sets before us, He will faithfully reward us, bountifully and abundantly. God will finance (***Isaiah 55:10, 2 Corinthians 9:10***...give seed to the sower) what we do for Him. He will finance it richly and plentifully, and the overflow will make us fat. GLORY HALLELUJAH !!! When we are faithful with what we do 'for Him' and 'in Him', we will receive thirty, sixty, one hundred fold return on whatever seed we sow. Keep in mind the reward/blessing of the faithful servant in the parable of the talents ***Matthew 25:14-29***, and ***Luke 19:11-27***.

A window of opportunity was opened before Jennifer to advance the kingdom of God. She seized the privilege to be a blessing, and blessings were heaped upon her.

(BEGINNING OF OUR CONVERSATION)

My divorce had just been finalized and I found out that my house payments were behind, about seven thousand dollars. That is why I was reasoning with God about the monthly gift He wanted me to give to you. I was in a bad enough financial fix already. However, when I was at your house and it was confirmed that I should do this, I stood on faith and was determined that I would do what God said.

I set within my heart, because of my divorce and my girls being so young (two and four years old), I wasn't going to just sit at home and rely on what is now called 'Family Independence Agency' for my provision. I wasn't going to depend on some fixed income to take care of me and my girls. I started at the Black Child and Family Institute searching for monies to go back to school. God blessed in that and the first time I went there I talked to who I believed was the director of the Institute. I don't remember his name, but I told him what I needed assistance with and he said that there was a new computer program that will take information from me about myself. It will evaluate pertinent information and then tell me according to my age and other statistics, where I should apply for funds, grants or scholarships.

When I went up to the second floor of the Institute to use this service, there was a class in progress and the instructor wouldn't let me in, but because the director was with me, I was admitted in the class to use this service.

I did get back a list of different places where I could apply for funds. When I finally sent off my request to receive information on how to apply for specific funds, I received a form back to fill out. On that form were two questions to be answered and these questions required quite lengthy answers.

I had just finalized my divorce, and mentally I was a mess. All I could think of was, Lord how am I going to answer these questions? I asked a friend over to point out to me how I should answer these questions. He looked over the form and was making what I thought were notes. Before I knew it he had answered all the questions for me. I submitted that application and I received a five thousand dollar award. Not a loan, an award that didn't have to be repaid. That was just the beginning.

I took that money and I applied to graduate school. The Lord blessed there and I got accepted into the master's degree program of Criminal Justice. The five thousand dollars went real fast and I realized that I didn't belong in that particular college. It didn't feel right and God always let you know when you're not in the right place. I went to apply to the school of Social Work and I needed more financial assistance to be accepted in that college. It just so happens that I had defaulted on a student loan back in 1982 when I attended college and I had forgotten about this loan over the years. I realized I was still responsible for the loan. When I called in to try to get monies, the scholarship people said no. God even worked in my getting accepted into this college (MSU) in the first place because the school of Criminal Justice and the school of Social Work are two different college's at MSU.

I was accepted, now I had to come up with the money and the scholarship people told me no, 'you were in default and in no way will we give you any more money'. I just prayed, Lord, you didn't bring me this far to leave me now. So after being told 'no' at least three times, I believed that the Holy Spirit told me to call back the fourth time. After you have been told no, no, no, then who else is there to go to, but God for direction. When I finally called back the fourth time, the man that was the director was on vacation. Someone else answered the telephone, and I said to her 'I know that I have been told this and that'…… (I don't really remember exactly what words I said, but I told her that I was really in need of monies). She said to me that he (the man I had talked to previously) couldn't reject my request based on my past loan record, and that she was going to grant me the money. How was I to know that he really could have given me the money when he constantly said no, no money? I had no way of knowing that he could have awarded me the funds. Thinking logically who would call back the fourth time unless the Holy Spirit told them to call again. God blessed in that step by granting me money for college. He granted me with more than enough money. (***You have not because you ask not James 4:2***).

God blessed me in other ways. For example, being a single parent, and going back to school full time wasn't an easy task. The Lord blessed in ways that it is hard to express. There were times that I had gotten homework that may as well been written in French because I didn't understand a word. All I could think was God, what am I going to do with these assignments? They were coming fast because I carried fourteen credit hours. God blessed through that. He sent people to me that could help me, and every assignment was turned in on time. There was lots of reading, at least three chapters a class per week and I had three classes. It was just a lot of work. How many people do you know that will come and say I will help you with your homework, and end up doing the entire assignment?

On May 2, 1997, the Lord blessed me to graduate with my Masters Degree in Social Work, and He is still Blessing me. He continues to bring spiritual and monetary blessings to me that just amaze me, they are just amazing.

I choose to believe that as I submitted and was faithful to His will, He blessed me.

(end of my conversation with Jennifer)

In all that God had called for us (me and Jennifer) to do for Him, we were faithful. It would have been easy for us to stop giving, and go about doing other things when I went out of town to care for my father. It is what we do for God when no one is around that defines our character.

At the time I moved, Jennifer had given me eight months of her promise. Jennifer was faithful to continue to the end of her charge. She let God know that He could trust her in all that He called her to do for Him. I let God know that He could trust me to the very end of my charge. In all that God chose us to do for Him we were faithful to Him, thereby exhibiting that we could be trusted to do His charges.

In one of my dreams in 1995, in a twilight state, as I was meditating on the goodness of the Lord, He told me to let Jennifer know that all she have received from God and all that was going on in her life;

(a) her home not being taken away from her,

(b) her children and her family being kept together,

(c) the people that God ushered into her life, to help her over her hurdles, and overcome the stumblingblocks, was the result of her faithfulness. God wanted me to tell her that all she had received in her endeavor to earn her Masters degree was a result of her faithfully sowing seed as God had commissioned her, a result, reward if you will, of her commitment to God. You hear me talk about commitment all the time. Either you are committed to God or you're not. There are no in betweens, no sometimes, no maybes, no perhaps.

    I want to tell you about her graduation ceremony. The school of Social Work didn't graduate with all of the other MSU graduates. Their graduation was a prestigious hooded ceremony. Ceremonial hooded robes were placed around their shoulders by their instructors, professors, or the alumni. They were presented honor ribbons around their necks and their hoods were placed on their heads. Their graduation exercise was held in their own school building and not with the nucleus of other graduates. After the certificates were awarded, there was a first rate reception. It was all very elegant.

    When God does something in your life, from the beginning to the end of that season in your life, he sends you in a first class lifestyle. Jennifer is now counseling within a prison system and she is faithful to witness to her clients about what God can do for them, if they just try Him and trust Him. For a time in her life, she wasn't sure where her degree in Criminal Justice would take her. God always has a specific plan and purpose for our lives.

    I guess by now you are asking, if I was as faithful as Jennifer, and if God is no respecter of persons, where is my harvest in all of this?

I'm glad you asked. I missed it in that season of my life. I was enrolled in a Bible College correspondence course about the same time as Jennifer was enrolled in MSU. When I went to care for my father, I allowed my flesh to rise up and interfere with my studies (that is another story). I had to care for my father as if Jesus Christ Himself was personally caring for him, and I did. I was in a perfect atmosphere and surrounding to continue and finish my Bible correspondence course. I didn't allow anyone or anything to take my focus off my care giving responsibilities; however, I did allow someone and something to rob me of my study and instruction time.

I have since repented, and asked the Lord to forgive me. I am now continuing with my correspondence course, and I will complete it. While I am doing just that, I will command the enemy that stole from me, by deception and lying, to restore unto me, my inheritance, my degree, and restore unto me sevenfold (according to ***Proverbs 6:30,31***) that which he took. This book is part of my harvest from sowing good seed into fertile ground.

We don't always know or recognize a particular harvest that comes from a particular seed. When we sow a car, and we receive a car we know the harvest. When we sow a coat, and we receive a coat, we know our harvest. When we sow love, and receive love, we know our harvest. When God instructs us in matters as mentioned above, I believe He is trying to place us into a position to receive from Him. That is why it is so important to be obedient, and be led by the Holy Spirit. When God manifests His grace to anyone, such as He did in the preceding accounts, there is no doubt who He is and how marvelous His works are.

Quite often when we sow financial seed into what we perceive as fertile ground, we are looking and expecting for an immediate and visible, tangible harvest, NOW. What God had given to Jennifer, and what He has in store for me, is something that no one can take from us. We can gleam wisdom from our journey. Wisdom that has brought us to the place we are now and it will last a lifetime.

Philippians 1:6...Being confident of this very thing, that he which hath begun a good work in you will perform it until the day of Jesus Christ:

James 4:2c

1 John 3:22

WISDOM FROM HEAVEN
(JAMES 3:13-18)

JAMES 3:13-18...

'WHO IS A WISE MAN AND ENDUED WITH KNOWLEDGE AMONG YOU? LET HIM SHOW OUT OF A GOOD CONVERSATION HIS WORKS WITH MEEKNESS OF WISDOM. BUT IF YE HAVE BITTER ENVYING AND STRIFE IN YOUR HEARTS, GLORY NOT, AND LIE NOT AGAINST THE TRUTH. THIS WISDOM DESCENDETH NOT FROM ABOVE, BUT IS EARTHLY, SENSUAL, DEVILISH. FOR WHERE ENVYING AND STRIFE IS, THERE IS CONFUSION AND EVERY EVIL WORK. BUT THE WISDOM THAT IS FROM ABOVE IS FIRST PURE, THEN PEACEABLE, GENTLE, AND EASY TO BE ENTREATED, FULL OF MERCY AND GOOD FRUITS, WITHOUT PARTIALITY, AND WITHOUT HYPOCRISY. AND THE FRUIT OF RIGHTEOUSNESS IS SOWN IN PEACE OF THEM THAT MAKE PEACE.'

LIFE'S LESSONS

As God was preparing me for retirement, there was what you would call a shake-up in management in the corporation where I had been employed for twenty years. I had always worked in the accounting department, and at this time I was bookkeeper.

Some of the managers/supervisors were being transferred out of the state to another branch of the same corporation and some of them were just moved around in the local branch. Some of the moves were promotions and some were not.

It seems to be the custom in large corporations that when a manager leaves a local branch, he/she hands out promotions, raises and bonuses to subordinates they are leaving behind.

(I didn't know that the Lord was getting me ready for retirement, I just knew that He was ushering into my life a new season.)

My branch manager and my immediate supervisor (not the same manager and supervisor in *Luke 6:35*) was being transferred to the home office with big, big promotions. They were feeling pretty good about their moves, so before they left they handed out a few promotions, and some raises. I received a raise, and one of my subordinates was given a promotion, above (in salary and title) where I stood in seniority.

The position to where she was promoted was created so that she would become a supervisor, over no department, still working in the section where I was supervising her. She had no training, experience or knowledge for the placement. I would have to train her. This was a repeat of the same situation that I was in when I was moved to this location.

I had ten years seniority over her with the corporation. I am aware that in some corporations longevity doesn't always count for advancement. However, there has been a history of unfair practices in this area with this company, and needless to say I was not happy. I was outraged! Not only would this move place her into a position over me, but also move her into a very lucrative benefit package.

When I went to my supervisors to ask why this junior employee was promoted above me, I was told that they had arbitrarily picked a title for her and didn't look for the requirements, benefit package or base salary. According to them their intention was to promote her to be equal with me. There was nothing that they could do about it now.

I did verbally make my dissatisfaction known with their decision, and with the corporation's compliance. I also let it be known in writing, by submitting a written grievance to the home office (I was salaried, no labor union). While I was waiting for a response from the home office concerning my written appeal, I attended a Friday all night prayer shut-in at my church.

As I was praying at the altar, I placed these two people (my manager and supervisor) on the altar. In my mind's eye I had to visualize them lying on the communion table that stood in front of the railing at the altar. I didn't know if a person should be placed on the communion table for sacrifice, even symbolically, but that was all I could think to do. I was so hurt and infuriated; all I could do was cry about the situation. I asked God to bless them and to show me how to handle this circumstance. I was angry and hurt and wanted to lash out at them, but I knew that wasn't the route to go. I knew what not to do, but I didn't know what to do. I prayed for them. I prayed good, and not evil. I prayed blessings, not curses. I prayed love, not hate.

WISDOM FOR GOD

In the midst of my crying out to God, I heard Him say that I should go to these two people and ask them to forgive me.

AS I MEDITATED ON GOD'S WORD

At that moment I think I wanted to shout and scream loud, loud, loud. I didn't know at the time, but the local branch had responded to my appeal, and I learned later that these two persons had been asked to give account of the decisions. I reasoned that I had done nothing unkind, nothing unfair to anyone; I didn't understand why I should be the one to ask them for forgiveness. I felt that I was the one that was exploited and embarrassed.

I asked God why I should ask them to forgive me when I was the one being hung out to dry, so to speak. I know I shouldn't have questioned the Holy Ghost, but I was really hurt, and I was thinking about myself. My next question was how do I ask the ones that had been unfair to me, to forgive me? I did repent for my questioning the Holy Ghost.

I was scheduled for vacation the following week and was glad because the manager and supervisor would be gone to their new positions the week I was due to return to work. Before that all night prayer shut-in, I had no intention of dropping by the office while I was on vacation to say good-by to them at their farewell luncheon.

I had to do some serious soul searching and role playing that weekend. I truly didn't want to go into the office and say farewell/good-by/God bless you, or nothing. At the altar on that Friday night I had my answer from God on what to do; now I had to figure out how to do it.

By Monday morning I had done some sincere repenting before God. I didn't want to do this task, but after asking God for help, and He sent His answer, what else could I do? I had to obey. I also knew that when I approached these two people, it would have to be in love. Before leaving the house on Monday morning, going to the office my prayer to God was:

'Father, I can't lie to you and say that love is in my heart for these two people. This is a hard task for me and I can't do it by myself. You know what is in my heart. Father, where you might have me to put love, there is obedience. Your Word says that if I ask anything in Jesus' name you will grant it to me, because I abide in you and your Word abides in me. I ask you to place in me, the love that you desire me to have and to share with my manager and my supervisor. Your Word also said that 'If any of you lack wisdom, let him ask of God, that giveth to all men liberally, and upbraideth not; and it shall be given him.' (James 1:5) I ask you for wisdom to say the words pleasing to you, and the love that you desire to be extended to your children.

(I know that love is a choice, a decision)

When I arrived at the office, everyone was surprised to see me. Everyone knew how I felt and how I was going to use my vacation to avoid saying good-by. When I showed up at the office there was wonderment in the atmosphere. The two that I had come to see was especially surprised.

My supervisor was in the office kitchen, and I asked her if I could speak to her alone at another area of the office. She said yes.

'I told her that I was sorry if I had hurt her in any way (by filing the written grievance with the home office) on the action that I had taken and I asked her to forgive me. I said that she would be gone from this local branch and I had to protect myself for future earnings. I impressed upon her that my intentions were not to hurt or harm her personally, but to protect myself. The action that I took was the only way I knew to handle the situation. I also told her that I pray that God would dispatch angels to watch over her as she entered her next step in the corporation. Again I asked her to forgive me.'

We embraced and both shed a few tears.

Then I went to my branch manager's office. I told him almost the same exact words (I had rehearsed them) that I said to my supervisor. 'Please forgive me if I hurt you in any way, but I acted in my own defense. My intention wasn't to attack you personally, but to protect myself for my future in this local branch, and with this corporation. Again, please forgive me if I hurt you in any way. May God bless you in your future positions with the corporation.'

We embraced and both shed a few tears. I said good-by, to both of them and left the office.

THANKS TO GOD

Father, in Jesus name, and in the power and presence of your precious Holy Spirit, you have shown me again the power of your love and the power of your forgiveness. You have taught me that I can do nothing of myself. That you are my strength, my shield and my buckler. That you can, and will speak for me by your Holy Spirit. I thank you for wisdom and grace. I'm so thankful and so grateful for your presence. Your grace is sufficient for me. Your Word says,

Psalm 91:1, 2...
He that dwelleth in the secret place of the most high shall abide under the shadow of the Almighty. I will say of the LORD, He is my refuge and my fortress; my God; in him will I trust.

Father, I thank you and I trust you to keep me safe.

Psalm 119:133...
Order my steps in thy word: and let not any iniquity have dominion over me.

I thank you for giving me the words that you would have me to say.

Psalm 141:3...
Set a watch, O LORD, before my mouth; keep the door of my lips.

I thank you for showing me forgiveness. Father, I thank you for my raise and promotion that was compensation for the previous action. You are my Strong Tower. I give you glory, I give you honor, I give you praise.

Father, I thank you for opening windows of heaven, and pouring me out blessings, that I have not room enough to receive. I thank you in the Name which is above every name, the name of Jesus Amen, and Amen.

James 3:13-18

ROBIN AND MY FATHER
(11 PETER 3:9)

11 PETER 3:9...
'THE LORD IS NOT SLACK CONCERNING HIS PROMISE, AS SOME MEN COUNT SLACKNESS; BUT IS LONGSUFFERING TO US-WARD, NOT WILLING THAT ANY SHOULD PERISH, BUT THAT ALL SHOULD COME TO REPENTANCE.'

It was the second week of December 1993, and I was going back to my hometown to attend a surprise bridal shower for my sister. As I was packing my van for what I thought was a weekend stay, the Holy Spirit impressed upon me to pack more clothing because I would be gone from my current residence for a longer period of time than a weekend. I didn't know how much longer, but I do know to obey those directives from the Holy Spirit, so I packed more clothes. I just had to wait for instructions from God.

I arrived in town the same day of the shower (Saturday); and after the shower (at my niece's house), I spent the night with my sister, at her house. The next day I attended a marriage dedication service for my sister and her future husband that was held at her church. They were going to Las Vegas to exchange the wedding vows. After the dedication/

Sunday service we went out to dinner, and since I told my family that I was going to be in town for a longer period of time than a weekend, they asked me whose house was I going to stay in. I could have stayed with my sister, but I knew she was making preparation for her wedding; and also she owned a business and had to run the operation of it until she left town. There were a number of other family members where I could have stayed, but with the holiday season I knew everyone would be extra busy.

My father, a widower, that would be 93 years old in February 1994, had been in a nursing home for about eight weeks, and no one was living in his house, so I decided to stay there. This was a good chance to air the house out and tidy up a bit while I waited to hear from God. My father had been widowed since 1990, and he lived by himself until he went into the nursing home. The house was not dirty, but it was cluttered with newspapers. I was later told that he continued the paper delivery to keep up with the days and months. He and my stepmother had lived in this house for more that 35 years before her death, and even though she had been deceased for a while, she was still very much there. My stepmother died in the hospital and not at home, but with the house being so cold (winter time) and empty it was really scary to me. No, I do not believe in ghost (the dead returning).

I began to visit my father at the nursing home daily. The personnel didn't monitor when or if he took his medication, so he took it when and if he wanted too. That wasn't very often, and as a result his senile dementia had worsened. He wasn't remembering to eat, and the attendants seemed not to care. There was no monitoring of his consumption of food or liquids. He had lost a lot of weight, and was confused most of the time. The year my stepmother died he had surgery for prostate cancer, so his health wasn't the best. He didn't know me or recognize me as his daughter.

The first few weeks that I stayed in his house, I slept on the couch in the living room, with all the lights on, all the time. It was now two weeks that I had been here and still not a word from God, why?

LIFE'S LESSONS

After a few weeks at my father's house, at about 3 am, I was awakened out of my sleep by Robin, one of my daughters' friends, whose car had stopped about one half block down the road. The temperature was below zero, and about five inches of snow was on the ground. It was clearly too cold to walk anywhere, especially that time of night. She wanted to use the telephone to call a friend to come and give her a ride home. I let her in to use the telephone, and while she waited for her ride we talked.

She said she lived a few blocks away and had noticed my car in the driveway the past few weeks. That's how she knew to come and knock on the door and ask for assistance. Robin and her sisters and my daughters had grown up together (35 years), and our families were very close. I couldn't seem to wake up completely to have a sound conservation with her, but I do remember asking her about her children, her mother, and her sisters. She began sharing with me how hurt she was with and about her son. He had gotten in trouble with the law, and was presently in jail. She mentioned other things going wrong in her life and she began to cry. My heart started melting for her, but I didn't know what to say or how to comfort her. I couldn't seem to completely wake up.

I received a telephone call from my sister about the second week of January, and she told me that she had received a call from the nursing home where my father was and that he had been taken to the emergency room with chest pains. I went to the emergency room and talked to the attending physician. He said my father didn't have a heart attack, but a bad case of indigestion. Because of his age and his heart condition (he wore a pacemaker) they wanted to keep him overnight for observation, and then he could go home. I asked the doctor what did he mean home? He said back to the nursing home.

WISDOM FROM GOD

When Robins ride arrived to take her home, as she was leaving the house, the Holy Spirit told me to witness to her. I took that to mean ask her if she had accepted Jesus Christ into her life and did she know Him as her Lord and Savior. If she hadn't invited Him into her life, did she want to do that tonight?

In the emergency room, when the doctor went to attend to other cases, the Holy Spirit told me that was why I was here. To take my father home, to his own personal residence. That I was to stay with him, care for him, and live with him in his own house. To God be the glory, I received my instructions.

AS I MEDITATED ON WISDOM FROM GOD

I was only half awake and didn't receive the full concept of the leading of the Holy Spirit until Robin had gotten into the car and rode away. I remember thinking that I will get her telephone number from my daughter the very next day and witness to her on the telephone. When I awoke the next morning, I remember very clearly the incident from the night before. I called my daughter and got Robin's phone number, but I didn't make calling her a priority on my list of things to do.

Three months later I went to the neighborhood grocery to purchase a money order, and as I entered the store Robin was at the check-out register ready to leave the store. I didn't see her until she called my name. As we exchanged hugs and hello's my spirit again quickened within me to witness to her. Well, I was in a hurry and I made a promise to myself that I would call her that night; or the next day for sure. (I didn't make the call.) One month later, on a Friday afternoon, my daughter called me on the telephone and told me that Robin had been at a friend's house for dinner, and while the food was cooking Robin went upstairs to take a short nap.

When dinner was ready, the friend called Robin to come down to eat. After a few minutes and no Robin, the friend went upstairs to awaken her and found her lifeless body in the bed. It was sudden. No warning. At that very moment when I heard what happened to Robin, I felt judgment had come into my life. (Later when I asked my daughter for more details, she said 'Mommy, I told you all of it on the phone.) I didn't hear a word she said after she told me Robin was deceased.

I remembered hanging up the phone, rushing to my bedroom, closing the door, falling on my knees and crying out to God to forgive me for not witnessing to Robin, about her salvation and forgive me for my disobedience. I repented to God. I don't know how long I cried and asked for forgiveness for my slothfulness, my laziness, but I promised God that I would never neglect the urgings of the Holy Ghost again concerning the things that He commissions me to do.

I heard this voice out of nowhere (but I really knew that it was on the inside of me) asking me why had I not heeded to the request of my father who wanted to be water baptized? Well, I began to cry even harder and was more repentant than before.

A few days later at Robin's home going, at the bottom of the program was a single, almost isolated statement that said:

'ROBIN ACCEPTED JESUS CHRIST INTO HER LIFE AND WAS WATER BAPTIZED.'

(The date of her conversion was included)

When I seen the by-line at the end of the program, it was as if God was saying, Carolyn, I forgive you. I know beyond a shadow of a doubt that that statement was for me. God was letting me know that when one of his people does not move at His request, there is always someone else that is ready and willing to move on His behalf.

God wishes that none perish. He always has a remnant to carry out His will. Not only was the by-line there, the ministers that officiated the service shared with everyone, the details of the exact night that Robin gave her life to Jesus Christ; and how she was water baptized at the same time.

When the doctor was free, I asked him if I could take my father home to his house instead of letting him go back to the nursing home. The doctor knew that I lived in another state, and he said the only way that he could go to his residence was that someone be with him 24 hours a day, 7 days a week. He impressed upon me very strongly that he couldn't be left alone for any length of time. His senile dementia had gotten worse and he would be harmful to himself if left alone. He wouldn't ever be able to live alone again. As the doctor was speaking, the Holy Spirit confirmed within me that I was to stay with him, care for him, and live with him in his own house.

During the time I cared for my father, he gained weight, his medication was regulated, and he wasn't as confused as before, although he still didn't recognize me as his daughter. He attended an adult day care program and we resumed church attendance. His senile dementia didn't get worse. All to the glory of God.

My father has always been faithful to attend church and to serve the Lord. He was a Sunday school teacher, church bus driver, auto and church mechanic, and whatever he could do to help his pastor, he did it. He also had been president of several of the church choirs, and at one time he formed his own choir 'The Reynolds Ensemble'.

Where I lived prior to coming here, I was a Bible teacher, superintendent and teacher for our Sunday school, and occasionally I had the privilege to share what God had put on my heart. It was not hard for either of us to get back into the practice of regular church attendance. That was the one constant in both our lives, our love for Jesus Christ.

I knew nothing about his Christian upbringing, except that he always attended church. I did know that his father was a preacher and taught in a one room classroom in Virginia. I also knew that he was raised 'Primitive Baptist'. In his adult life he attended a missionary Baptist Church. I was a member of another denomination, but I did take him to his church where he was a member. Some people he knew, and most he didn't remember, so I didn't feel bad when we started to attend a church where I was more comfortable. The services were quite different from what he was used to, but he really enjoyed the praises and worship.

He attended the adult Sunday school class with a friend of mine that was aware of his state of mind.

One Sunday after class my friend told me that my father had requested to be water baptized. I said ok, but I let it slip out of my mind. On 2 other occasions, I was told that my father had asked to be water baptized. That made a total of 3 requests, and I don't know why I was so laid back about the matter. I guess I took for granted that he had already been water baptized and that he couldn't remember. When the Holy Spirit reminded me about my father's desire to be water baptized, I was truly convicted. When I repented and accepted the forgiveness of Jesus Christ, I made arrangements with my pastor for my father to be water baptized on Sunday, in 2 days. He was submerged in water September of 1994 at the age of 93 ½. (I have pictures to prove it.)

I have no idea what the belief is concerning water baptism for primitive Baptist. Only God knows the heart and mind of His children, and it wasn't for me to conclude that my father had already been water baptized. I realize that the request for water baptism was coming from God and not just the utterance from my father, and not just an utterance from his dementia. There are many instances where a person has confessed with their mouth and believed in their hearts that Jesus Christ is Lord, has invited Him into their lives, and yet it was impossible to be water baptized, such as the thief on the cross next to Jesus.

John 3:5...
Jesus answered, Verily, verily, I say unto thee, Except a man be born of water and of the Spirit, he cannot enter into the kingdom of God.

God is loving; He is just; He is forgiving; He is full of grace and mercy. As I said before, only God knows the hearts of men, and the intents of the hearts (***Hebrews 4:12***) of His people. When God commissions us or ordains us to do a specific task for Him, It's not up to us to figure out the time frame in which to comply. Tomorrow is not promised. We are to be expedient and ready to move into God's arena with action to carry out His desires, His wishes, His way. He doesn't force us to receive or accept His good pleasure, or His blessings. He is faithful and generous in His forgiveness and with His rewards.

THANKS TO GOD

Father, I thank you for your sacrifice on Calvary. Because of your sacrifice, my sins were nailed to your cross (***Colossians 2:14***). Thank you for forgiving me my sin of slothfulness, and thank you for the quickening of your Holy Spirit within me to adhere to your will and to your desires. Father, I thank you for the God ordained encounters that you placed on my path. I thank you for divine connections and divine appointments.

Thy word have I hid in my heart, that I might not sin against thee. (Psalm 119:11)

I give you praise, all honor and glory belongs to you. Jesus I give you thanks, and I magnify your Name.

Jesus I love you, and your Name, which is above every Name, the precious Name of Jesus I will lift up and glorify.

My father being water baptized September 23, 1994

II Peter 3:9

DREAM – MAY, 1992
(PROVERBS 4:1)

PROVERBS 4:1...
'HEAR, YE CHILDREN, THE INSTRUCTION OF A FATHER, AND ATTEND TO KNOW UNDERSTANDING'.

I was walking with a child on a sandy beach. It was a clear day, sun shinning, not hot, but a warm breeze. To my right a few yards away was a dry grassy area, not sandy or very tall. The child (10 or 11 years old) was walking on my left side, between me and the ocean. The ocean was very calm and serene, and we were just walking and talking.

About 20 feet out on the ocean (to the left of the child) was a large and fat man lying on his back, floating. He was so fat, it appeared that he couldn't get up if he wanted. His belly was high above his body, like a large ball or balloon, and he was looking up to the sky. He was floating there with his legs stretched out in front of him, and his feet were spinning, fast, vertically. He wasn't moving one way or another. His arms were stretched out to his sides with his palms turned upward. It was as if he was anchored and couldn't move, although in my dream I knew that that wasn't the case. There wasn't a ripple in the water coming from his feet spinning. There wasn't even a splash of water of any kind. The scene was entirely motionless, except for his feet. His head was toward the direction that we were walking, and his feet to the back of us. If he stood up, he would face us.

Then his left arm and hand began going in and out of the water the way an oar would if someone would be rowing a boat. His arm and hand were going straight up and straight down instead of in a directional movement. This was a continuous motion until one time when his arm and hand went down into the water, he brought a small child (seemed less than one year old) up out of the ocean. As he brought up the child on his upward swing, he tossed the child to the child that was walking beside me. The child that was walking beside me caught the little one and immediately handed him to me. I noticed that the little one was not breathing, so I began to pat him on his back, firmly holding him high on my left shoulder, hoping that he would catch his breath and start to breathe. He didn't. So I laid the child down on his back in the grassy area, in a position to administer life saving techniques, and I began to apply those methods (for a drowning person). Not mouth to mouth resuscitation, but when you straddle the body and manually pump the torso/trunk to clear the blocked air passages. In a very short time this worked, and the little one turned his head to his left side and coughed up what seemed to be wet sawdust, very runny and then he started to breathe. I picked him up and resumed our walk on the beach, and then I woke up.

I didn't know what that dream meant, so I said out loud, 'Jesus, what does that dream mean?' and immediately I went back to sleep.

I began the very same dream from the beginning, only now Jesus was walking beside me on my right side. He said 'you see that man out there on the ocean, he is bogged down with problems, worries and matters that he can't solve. He is trying to resolve them by doing things, and all he is doing is spinning his wheels (feet). He isn't moving anywhere. He's not even making ripples in the water (life). He isn't accomplishing anything and his wheels keep spinning faster and faster. He can't seem to help himself, so he is stretching himself out to help someone else. The one that he pulled out of the water was drowning (in life), and he rescued him out of the water and tossed him to you. The young child walking beside you was closer to the water so she caught him and handed him to you.'

I asked why then couldn't I help him by patting him on the back so that he could catch his breath and begin to breathe? I asked why did I have to apply life saving skills before he could breathe?

Jesus said 'Because holding him and patting him on his back would only help him to catch his breath, but wouldn't save his life. The little one needed someone to help save his life. He needed more than a temporary fix. He needed sustaining life pumped into his body. He needed debris (strongholds) and blocking particles (imaginations) pumped out (removed), and his air passages unblocked (deliverance) so that he can breathe sustaining life into his body. He needed someone to assist him and show him how to put on the whole armor of God'.

I said, oh, now I understand.

I had this dream in May of 1992, and God supernaturally brought retirement to me effective December, 1992. I didn't know in May that God was preparing me to work for Him full time. His message was that people drowning in life, who come into/before/on my path, I am to assist them breathe in life, being led by the Holy Ghost. His message was that He had a specific work for me to do for Him. The child walking beside me on my left is someone that has been placed in my life to assist me. (I don't know how I knew the genders of the children in my dream. It was a dream.)

I have had other dreams that I didn't understand, and when I asked for understanding, I was enlightened. This is the one and only dream/vision (to this date) that Jesus Himself appeared by my side walking with me. At my request He walked with me step by step, giving me understanding. I have recognized Jesus in other dreams and visions, but not like this.

When we get to a place in our lives where it seems that we're not accomplishing anything, not with ourselves and not in the kingdom of God we are to stretch/extend ourselves out to some/others and help them. We should be aware of our actions, or non-action; be discerning about our surroundings and help those around us. Assist those that God have put on our paths. We're to take our eyes off ourselves and our circumstances and demonstrate compassion (love in action), to others. We can be used by God when we look to Him for direction. He will use us for His good when we learn to see Him in all of His creation. We should determine to offer our bodies as living sacrifices, holy and acceptable unto God, which is and should be our reasonable service. When we refuse to be conformed to this world, but be transformed by our minds being renewed in, by and through Christ Jesus, then we will begin to know that good and acceptable and perfect will of God (***Romans 12:1, 2***).

Our ultimate goal should be to seize the opportunities that are put before us to further the kingdom of God.

Isaiah 6:8
Also I heard the voice of the Lord, saying, Whom shall I send, and who will go for us? Then said I, Here am I; send me.

PROVERBS 4:1

A SPECIFIC WORD
(ISAIAH 54:2, 3)

ISAIAH 54:2, 3...
'ENLARGE THE PLACE OF THY TENT, AND LET THEM STRETCH FORTH THE CURTAINS OF THINE HABITATIONS: SPARE NOT, LENGTHEN THY CORDS, AND STRENGTHEN THY STAKES; FOR THOU SHALT BREAK FORTH ON THE RIGHT HAND AND ON THE LEFT; AND THY SEED SHALL INHERIT THE GENTILES, AND MAKE THE DESOLATE CITIES TO BE INHABITED'.

(This scenario happened in the winter of 1995. I am recording this in the summer of 1998, and His 'Specific Word' is still ringing loud and clear in my spirit. It is continuously fresh manna to my spirit.)

November of 1995, I was facing a dilemma, a juncture, a fork in the road so to speak, in my journey of life. I had to make a choice between two roads or paths to take. In each direction stood one of my daughters; each one about to make major decisions in their lives. The indecision of what road to take wasn't with them, but with me; and because of timing and finances, it seemed that I couldn't travel both paths. I needed a 'Specific Word' from God.

One road would take me to Phoenix, Arizona. My second oldest daughter was moving her family from Ohio to Arizona. Her family consisted of herself (a divorcee), an 18 year old son, and a 7 year old daughter. The company where she was employed was relocating employees to Arizona to open and staff a new branch office in Phoenix. She had contemplated about this move for three years. Now the plans were coming off her drawing board and was becoming a reality in her life. It had been a long time since such happiness and excitement, and the feeling of freedom had filled her life. She so looked forward to this move.

She would be driving a moving van loaded with furniture and appliances from a two bedroom townhouse. Hitched to the van would be a trailer carrying her car. She would be driving a distance close to two thousand miles by herself. (Her son didn't have his driving permit.) She had never driven on the highway in her life, and as much as she looked forward to this venture with confidence and enthusiasm, I knew that she had no idea what to expect. I believed that she had no conscious concept of what it would take physically and emotionally to make such a journey by herself (with God, yes). I knew the stamina it would take to drive, pulling almost twenty four feet of equipment around winding roads, up and down mountains, in and out of all kinds of terrain, driving day and night, mostly night (no daylight savings time, this time of year). She had traveled out of town before, however, I had always done all the driving, or we went by motor coach and air to our destination.

The road that she was about to drive was a road that I had driven in 1970. I and my four daughters got into our 1963 Ford Thunderbird and drove from Ohio to California. That was my first experience of highway driving, so I am speaking from knowledge. It was a pleasure vacation in the summer (lot's of daylight driving) and in a small car. We had no particular schedule when it came to duration of time. If you haven't driven on the highway in your home state, you can't fathom what it would be like to drive across the country.

It wasn't a matter if she could do it; I knew she could. I felt that she wasn't prepared for the enormity of such an undertaking. I also knew that spiritually, God had already set her time, in Him, for her to do this. I wanted so very badly to go with her. I wanted to let her know that I supported her in her decision, and that I believed in her. I wanted to help her drive and be adult company for her. I was worried for her; she wasn't. Mentally, emotionally, and financially (her company financed the move) in her mind she was ready. As much anxiety as I had for her, I would be doing the very same thing that she was doing had I the opportunity when I was in her season of life.

We had no relatives in Phoenix, and she had no way of contacting the co-workers she knew that had already relocated to that area. Once she reached her destination who was going to help her? So my concern wasn't only her driving in unfamiliar territory, but when she reached her destination, who was going to help her unload the van and move her into a second floor, two bedroom apartment? This relocation was to happen in two weeks and I hadn't received word from the Lord if I should accompany her. I hadn't received my 'Specific Word'.

The other road led to Lansing, Michigan. My eight year old granddaughter was to have her tonsils removed in a few days. Her mother and I had lived together since she was born, so you could say that I had a part in raising her, except for the time I spent in Ohio carrying for my father. My family in Michigan had counted on me being there for support and encouragement. I know that a tonsillectomy isn't considered major surgery to the general populace, but when it comes home or to a member of our family, we think of all sorts of complications happening, and it is a major event.

Even though I haven't gone into as much detail about the second road, doesn't make it any less significant in my life. Both of these circumstances were major milestones in our lives, and major choices for me to make. There was also another situation that factored into my decision, but God hasn't released me to reveal/share that at this time.

As the time approached for both events to take place, I hadn't heard from God. I had to wait for Him and His direction. I was still waiting for my 'Specific Word'.

One Sunday evening church service, a visiting evangelist/prophetess was the main speaker. As she began to deliver her prepared message, her thoughts kept wandering to another passage of Scripture. After about the fourth time that she drifted off her topic and notes, she said; 'for some reason the Holy Spirit isn't letting me deliver what I have prepared. So I will go to the passage of Scripture where He is taking me and that is ***Esther 4:16b, if I perish, I perish***. This message is for someone here. The Lord has a word for someone that is wrestling with a decision and this is your answer from God'.

I knew that the Holy Spirit was talking to me. I don't remember any of the message. I can't tell you anything that she said, but my spirit received my answer from God. A settling had come into my being. I was to go to Michigan to be with my granddaughter when she had her tonsils removed.

When I left church that night, I stopped by my daughter's house and I shared with her how strange our evening service was. This was the daughter that was preparing to move to Arizona. I told her that I knew the message was for me, but I would have to wait until morning to go to the bank for gas money. She handed me twenty dollars and asked if that would get me to Michigan. I said yes, and went home to pack a few things. The twenty dollars went into the gas tank and there was no money left over. This trip was purely a faith journey.

The surgery was scheduled for Tuesday morning, and I traveled on Monday. I hadn't been in Michigan for a while and arriving there on Monday afternoon afforded my daughter, granddaughter and me the time to talk and bond spiritually before the surgery.

Tuesday morning we checked into the outpatient surgery department of the hospital and was escorted to the floor and room where patients are prepped for the procedure.

The nurses came in to draw blood from my granddaughter, and to outfit her with an IV, so that they could administer medication for and during surgery. I didn't know that she had a fear of needles. I found out. It took four adults to hold her down after she saw the needle, to no avail. That was an experience I hope I never have to go through again in life. She fought, screamed and hollered so loud, other people on the floor thought she had a terrible accident there in the room. The nurse's were never able to draw her blood. The doctor's decided to wait until she was in the operating room to give her something to calm her down, and then take the specimen they needed. He felt that she would be more manageable to all the other pre-op work up. Her mother was going to be with her in surgery (I'm not sure how hospital's handle that), and I was told to go to the out-patient waiting room until surgery was over. When she went into the recovery room, they would call down and let me know the status of her condition, how long she would be in recovery, and when I could come up to see her.

I gathered up our things and went to the waiting room for my call, which I was told would be about one and one half hour. I got a cup of coffee, settled into my seat and relaxed to read a book that I had brought to catch up on my reading.

After twenty minutes, and four pages into my book, my daughter came into the waiting room and told me that the doctor decided not to do the surgery. I asked why? She said the physician thought that my granddaughter was too excited for the surgery. They could give her enough medication to calm her down completely and perform the tonsillectomy, however, after care could be a problem and cause complications in treatment because of her fear of needles and her uncertainty of what was happening. The doctor's talked it over and decided to wait, maybe two years when she was older. They felt that two years would make a difference in her acceptance for the procedure. My daughter had come down to get my granddaughters clothes, so that she could get dressed and we could go home.

I was stunned. I was shocked, baffled or something. I just sat there. I couldn't move or think. I talked with God. I was attempting to make some sense of the situation. Out of the entire equation, I was the only one transplanted to here in this state. My daughter and granddaughter lived here. The hospital is always here. The doctor's are always here. My absence wouldn't have stopped the surgery and my presence had no direct bearing on any of the events of this morning. My question to God was,

'Why was I here? Why was there such a wrestling in my spirit to come here at this time? From the events of this morning, the doctor's didn't know in advance that the actual operation wouldn't be performed. My daughter and granddaughter didn't know that everything would be cancelled. I didn't know that the surgery wouldn't take place. God, you are the only One that knew for sure that she would keep her tonsils. Because you are all knowing, you knew everything that would happen this morning. God, you and you alone know the beginning and the end of all things. You are the only One who knows what will take place in between those two points. My only reason for being here at this time is for this operation. In this scenario I am the only displaced person here. Why? Why am I here?'

Because of the events of that Tuesday morning, I knew that God had brought me here to receive a 'Specific Word' from Him. I had no idea when or from what source it would come. I knew I had to live each day as usual, and be intensely and spiritually attuned to the voice of God. I also knew that It wasn't time to go home because God hadn't put the money into my hands for the return trip (my bank in Ohio did not have a branch here). My credit union anytime card wouldn't work at any of the money stations here, so I had to wait.

I went shopping and bought me a pair of shoes and a top. I called a friend of mine and she offered to buy dinner for all of us. She brought chicken dinners over, we ate together and had a wonderful time of fellowship. The Holy Spirit captured those few hours as we related to her the events of the past few days. After my friend left, I thought about;

Isaiah 40:31, But they that wait upon the LORD shall renew their strength; they shall mount up with wings as eagles; they shall run, and not be weary; and they shall walk, and not faint.

As I meditated on what that meant specifically to me, I was led to read,

Lamentations 3:25, The LORD is good unto them that wait for him, to the soul that seeketh him.

I praised Him in,

Psalm 27:14; 62:5, Wait on the LORD: be of good courage, and he shall strengthen thine heart: wait, I say, on the LORD. My soul, wait thou only upon God; for my expectation is from him.

Then when I read **Habakkuk 2:3**, I found real comfort in waiting.

For the vision is yet for an appointed time, but at the end it shall speak, and not lie: though it tarry, wait for it; because it will surely come, it will not tarry.

Wednesday daytime was a day as usual. That evening I went to Bible study at the church where I attended before going to Ohio. I was late, so I lingered afterwards to say hello to the pastor. Before I could say anything, he said 'the Lord gave me a word for you'. We went to the front of the sanctuary, and he turned in his Bible to **Isaiah 54:2, 3**.

Since he didn't know what was happening with me in this season of my life, he shared with me what that Scripture spoke to him. Then he added, I should ask God what that passage means to me.

As soon as the pastor read that particular Scripture out loud, and before he had a chance to expound upon it, the words came into my spirit, 'now you can go home'. After the pastor explained more on those two verses, and I received them as my 'Specific Word' from God, I went back to my daughter's house and shared with her what happened that night at Bible Study. I told her that in my spirit I knew why I had to come to Michigan. She wasn't aware of the wrestling that I had within myself about her sister's move to Arizona and about my granddaughter's surgery.

God can, and He will speak to us anytime and anyplace. There are times that we must be removed from our immediate environment to recognize that God is speaking to us individually, and that it is a 'Specific Word' that He desires just for us to receive from Him. God takes us out of our familiar zones to be alone with Him.

There are many accounts in the Bible where God has taken His people to a particular place to hear His voice. It's kind of like a shaking up. If we're not shaken, and shaken good, we don't hear with our spiritual ears. God had to take me out of my comfort zone in a jerking manner, so to speak, to get my undivided attention, NOW. He had to isolate me into His presence, so that I could hear HIM; and receive from HIM. When God directs us to go to an exact place or location in the natural, most likely it is to get us out of our comfort zone and ignite us to be propelled to go to another dimension, spiritually. A place where God can minister to us, in Him, on a level higher than where we have been.

2 Kings 2:1-11:
Elijah had to go to a certain place, to cross the Jordan River, by Jericho, and go to a specific location before he was translated to heaven.

1 Samuel 17:32-51:
As a shepherd boy, David slew the lion and the bear on his home territory. He had to go to the 'Elah Valley', outside of the city of Bethlehem, as a warrior to slay Goliath.

Luke 2:3-7:
In obedience to the decree, Joseph and Mary had to go from Nazareth to Bethlehem to be taxed. Jesus was born in the very town prophesied for His birth.

Acts 9:1-6:
Saul had to leave his place of comfort and earthly power to meet Jesus on the Damascus Road before he could receive his instructions, and his name changed to Paul (*Acts 13:9*).

When God birth's a desire in our heart/spirit to go to a precise area, go there. He wants to speak to us. He knows where we will hear Him, and He knows when and where we will receive His Word. He knows from whom, and from where we need to be removed; and He knows to whom and to what location to transplant us, for us to acknowledge that it is God that we hear. He loves us so much that He allows us to become uncomfortable, just to get our undivided attention. He is waiting to propel us to another dimension, greater and closer to our destiny in Him.

At that particular juncture in my life, I desired to be a significant part of my children's lives. My desire to be an intimate part of their lives would eventually have caused conflict in our relationships, and in our families. I can see that now. Had I gotten what I wanted at that time, dependency on me would have become a clinging, stifled and unloving family tie; depending on each other instead of relying solely on Jesus. The Bible let's us know that to be supportive in another's life, we must pray for them, and let them go, in love. I had to enlarge my place of spiritual abode; to let God fill me with more of Him. I don't own my children. They belong to God, and I am a steward for Him. I had to trust Him to do for them, what I'm not capable of doing. In allowing God to fill me with more of Him, I could let my children be all that they can be in Christ Jesus.

The bonding of love, respect, and most of all trusting in God to handle all of our affairs, put me at peace. I trusted that Jesus would do all that He said He would do, and I know that,

2 Corinthians 1:20, For all the promises of God in him are yea, and in him Amen, unto the glory of God by us.

I trusted that Jesus would develop in my children's lives and that He would manifest mightily in all that they do. As we lift Jesus up, God will be glorified, and His presence will occupy every facet of our lives. As a witness and a testimony to our love for Him, and our trust in Him, the finished work of Jesus on His cross (***Colossians 2:14b***), we can love one another as we let go and grow more in the love and nurturing of Jesus Christ. I realized that I had to let go of all the anxiety that I was clinging to about my daughter's move. I had to let her go by herself, and trust that Jesus was going all the way with her. I had to place her in the arms, hands and the total and complete care of Almighty God. Not only her, but all my children, my seed. I had to depend solely on God for all that they needed and for all that they will ever need. I let go of all the fretfulness, the weight, the concern, and yes, the worry that I was embracing. I depended on God to perform His Word according to **Romans 8:28,**

And we know that all things work together for good to them that love God, to them who are the called according to his purpose.

1) all things of God; 2) all things of prayer; 3) and all things of intercession, according to the will of God.

When I finished sharing with my daughter all that was in my spirit that night, I told her that also I knew that I could go home. The banks were closed and neither one of us had cash, however, she did have a large water container almost filled with coins. We counted out twenty dollars and then retired for the night. Thursday morning I used part of the cash for gas and the other to fill a prescription, and then headed home. It was a four hour drive that was energized and electrified with the presence of God traveling with me. I almost wished that the drive could have lasted longer.

Nevertheless, there always comes a time when we must work the work of Christ Jesus. There is a time to pray, and there is a time to act on the fruit of our prayer life. Even though I received the fact that I wasn't to accompany my daughter on her travel, the unloading and moving into her apartment lingered in my mind.

At that time I was a licensed minister of a particular denominational church organization, and an updated manual was recently published and distributed to all who were licensed in that denomination. The listing included the names, address's and telephone numbers of all the Bishop's, Elder's, and Ministers in the world. They were listed by city, state, region and country. I was prompted in my spirit to use this reference book to our advantage. In the geographical location where my daughter was to reside, I began to telephone the licensed person's listed in that area. The first person (first name on the list) I called was an Elder. I introduced myself, my affiliation with the organization, my pastor and my Bishop, and how I happened to get his name and telephone number. I explained to him the situation that my daughter would face when she arrived at her destination, and I asked him if he could be of assistance or direct me to someone who could help her. All he said was 'I can't be of service to you or your daughter.' I thanked him for his time and moved down the list.

The second name was a Bishop. I called him, introduced myself, my pastor, my Bishop, etc. He immediately said that he could and would help. This is what I heard him say:

'The church that I pastor has a moving company franchise and they have encountered other situations like this. Because Arizona is a somewhat transit state, they have helped other people before. He gave me his church telephone number, his home address and phone number, and his pager number. He also gave me an alternate name and phone number of a church member to call in case he couldn't be reached. I was to relay this information to my daughter when she called me en route to Arizona. He said for her to call when she arrived and he would send a crew of workers out to help her unload and move into her apartment. There would be no charge for this. From time to time they donate their services as the Lord directs them'.

That is what I heard on the telephone that night talking to the Bishop.

When my daughter called me after the third night of her journey, she shared with me the problems that she had encountered. The truck that she leased in Ohio had broken down two times. The first time, she called the (1-800) number that the leasing company had provided her with. They came to where she was and repaired the truck. The second time the truck broke down, it couldn't be repaired. She had to be towed to the trucking company, where they proceeded to unload and reload her into another truck. She was told that this one would take her to her destination. She called me from a motel where the leasing company had secured a room for her and her family for the night. I gave her the information on how to contact the Bishop when she arrived in Arizona, and relayed his message to her.

When she got to her destination she called me to let me know that she had made it there safe. All the glory is to God Almighty!!! She said the second truck had also broken down on the highway in New Mexico. She and her son had to unhitch the trailer that carried her car, release the car from the trailer, leave the truck on the side of the road and she drove her family ninety nine miles to her apartment. By the time she had called me, she had already called the Bishop and he had already sent help to assist her. She relayed to me later that three men came to help her. They took her and her family out to eat, and then they drove her back to where the truck had stopped, ninety nine miles, back to New Mexico. One of the men managed to start the truck and drove it ninety nine miles to Arizona, while another one of the men drove her car following the truck. They unloaded the truck and moved her into her apartment. They accompanied her to the leasing company where she returned the truck, she filed a claim with the leasing company for the broke truck, and then they brought her back to her apartment.

When we finished talking on the telephone, I praised God for His grace and His mercy. I thanked Him for His traveling angels that watched over my family. I thanked Him for His divine protection toward my daughter and His servant. She is a born again Christian.

She also told me that the church did not have a moving company. The move that they had was a 'MOVE OF GOD'. When we are in distress, God allows us to hear what we need to hear. I needed to hear that God had already provided safety and security for my daughter at the end of that particular road for her. He knew I needed comfort, as well as she needed to know that God's angels were perched waiting for God to summons them. *Hebrews 1:14* says; *Are they not all ministering spirits, sent forth to minister for them who shall be heirs of salvation?*

Yes, there are ministering spirits waiting to be sent forth. They were ready to rise to the occasion and give to her all that God had reserved for her. God is waiting to send help. He knew that I needed to hear what I thought the Bishop was saying that night. God knew I needed to hear secure comforting words that night.

The Bishop and his congregation were truly touched by the hand of God in this situation. All of their assistance was rendered to a family in distress. Neither the Bishop, nor his people knew me or my family. We knew no one in common except Jesus Christ. All of this was done without prying questions, or a formal application. It was done out of pure love. God was truly in charge of the entire move.

I have known the goodness of our Lord and Savior. I have tasted and seen that He is good *Psalm 34:8*. I know of His loving kindness. I know of His grace and His majesty. I know the intensity of His love for His own. I know how far He will reach to touch His precious ones. I am always in awe of His marvelous works, how His presence and His might reaches out to me. I'm so grateful, and I'm so thankful for

His sacrifice on the cross. I'm thankful how He uses others to hearken to His directives, and how others are willing to be humble and used by God. I did take the time to call the Bishop and thank him for his graciousness. My daughter kept in contact with him for a season; and still does from time to time. They are in our prayerful thoughts.

I had a chance to visit my family in Phoenix in December, 1996. We visited the Bishop's church for a Sunday morning service. After service I approached the Bishop to introduce myself, and to thank him personally. Before I could say anything he told me he knew who I was. It had to be the Holy Spirit. At the time that I was shaking his hand, I received a 'Specific Word' from God for him. It was that because of him extending himself in selfless love toward helping my daughter, whatever that thing was that he desired, it would come forth, in the name of Jesus. He looked puzzled and he didn't tell me what it was that he desired, but we serve a God that loves, and is faithful and true. I was also introduced to the three men that helped her. As I shook their hands, I received the same 'Specific Word' for them, and I shared that with each one. One of the men walked with a profound limp, assisted by a cane, and God used him in that crisis. God can use all of us if we're willing to be used.

I haven't heard of anything from, or about that Bishop or those three gentlemen in recent times. I know God and I know some things are just for a season. God will do anything and everything to get a 'Specific Word' to you. Are you listening for your 'Specific Word?'

GOD IS LOVING. GOD IS FAITHFUL.
GOD IS TRUTH.

ISAIAH 54:2, 3

PRAYER PARTNERS
(GALATIANS 6:2)

GALATIANS 6:2...
'BEAR YE ONE ANOTHER'S BURDENS, AND SO FULFILL THE LAW OF CHRIST'

LIFE'S LESSONS

Prayer partners are very special. The concept came from God, and I'm sure we all want to give Him thanks for praying partners. When we are partnered with someone, we don't always know (some exceptions) what God is working out in our lives, or in the lives of others.

A good example of partner's in agreement is in ***Exodus 17:12***. When Amalek fought with Israel in Rephidim, and Moses, Aaron and Hur went up to the top of the hill to view the battle, Moses' hands were heavy from holding them up as Israel prevailed. Aaron and Hur sat Moses on a stone, and each one of them held up his hands steady as Israel conquered their enemy, until the going down of the sun. The three of them came into total agreement and was rendered victorious in battle.

Deuteronomy 19:15b,
...at the mouth of two witnesses, or at the mouth of three witnesses, shall the matter be established.

Matthew 18:19, 20,
Again I say unto you, That if two of you shall agree on earth as touching any thing that they shall ask, it shall be done for them of my Father which is in heaven. For where two or three are gathered together in my name, there am I in the midst of them.

I personally know of a unique case of prayer partnering, where two persons have been praying together for twenty seven years on a daily basis, in town and out of town. This union is rare and very special. There are also persons like me that have had many praying partners. I have found that both circumstances work for God.

When God takes me from glory to glory, or season to season, my prayer partner may change. Sometimes a partner is close for months, sometimes for years. God is in total control of choosing the partner and the time duration. The partner is never dropped from my prayer list.

April, 1996 God supernaturally brought into my life an acquaintance as my prayer partner and I was truly puzzled (we think we know what God is up to; WRONG).

As I began to pray for that person, a hunger for intercession took place in my heart. We all should have a desire to pray for one another, but this hunger was different, this was anointed of God and I knew it.

My partner began to call me and share how a relative had brought very damaging false accusations against him and how they went so far as to hire an attorney and bring legal actions against him. He had been served with a summons to appear in court to answer the charges. The news media (radio, TV, newspapers) had taken the matter and capitalized on it and was blowing it all out of proportion.

The courts had taken charge of his finances to the extent that he couldn't purchase gas for his car, or food for his family without the courts consent. He was even held incarcerated overnight when he went to answer the summons. The next morning upon his release, TV cameras and reporters were present to get a story.

He shared with me the pain, distress and embarrassment of not having finances for his family, especially at the holiday season (Thanksgiving, Christmas, and New Years). The burden of not being able to provide decent meals and some gifts was almost unbearable. He was to appear before a judge in two days and he had already been warned by his attorney that the law enforcement had decided not to allow him to come to court on his own. They were going to come to his house to arrest him to make him an example for others and embarrass him in front of his family and neighbors. Also the news media would be present. As he was speaking the Holy Spirit began interceding.

Romans 8:27,
And he that searcheth the hearts knoweth what is the mind of the Spirit, because he maketh intercession for the saints according to the will of God.

I didn't accuse him of anything, interrogate him, or attempt to intimidate him by asking a lot of incriminating or probing questions. I listened, and I prayed with him at the end of our conversation. I prayed after we hung up the telephone. I prayed fervently that night. My prayer with him was that the power and the presence of the Holy Spirit would rest, rule and abide with him in the days to come and through all of the trouble that he was to encounter. I prayed in the name which is above every name, the name of Jesus. My private prayer had to be led by the Holy Spirit on how and what to pray.

My favorite time with Jesus is when I'm on the walking/jogging path. As I ended my secret prayer that night, I made a mental note to myself that I would pray for him and the situation on my morning walk at the exact time of the hearing. Then I fell asleep.

WISDOM FROM GOD

The morning of his court appearance, as I was putting on my walking shoes, the Holy Spirit told me to drive over to his (my prayer partner) house and pray walking and encircling his house. I was to not only pray for him, but his family members individually, his house, the ground and areas surrounding his property.

AS I MEDITATED ON GOD'S WORD

This wasn't the first time that I actually felt the burden of what my prayer partner was going through, but the weight of it was different. Up to this point I hadn't been to his home, although I did know where it was located. So myself, my car, and what I would be doing might be considered strange to his neighbors. I knew without a doubt that it was the Holy Spirit that was directing me, and I knew that I had to obey the prompting in me. So I did, after I said Holy Spirit I trust you to truly guide each and every step. I knew that his neighbors would be watching (that's what neighbors do). This situation was a daily news item. When I arrived at his house, I started with;

'Heavenly Father, I come in the name of Jesus and in obedience to your command. It is written;

Psalm 37:23,
The steps of a good man are ordered by the LORD: and he delighteth in his way.

I trust you to guide these steps and the words you have written, for they have stood the test of time. It is written;

Psalm 119:89.
For ever, O LORD, thy word is settled in heaven.

I carried my Bible and recited out loud the words of God; and I personalized them to the occasion as I was led by the Spirit of the Lord.

These are the Scriptures I read out loud:

Isaiah 54:17; 2 Corinthians 10:4, 5; Ephesians 6:11-20; Malachi 3:10, 11; John 15:7, 8; 2 Corinthians 12:9; 5:17, 18; Isaiah 55:11, 12; Nehemiah 8:10; Jeremiah 1:12; I ended reading with *Romans 8:26.*

I covered my prayer partner, his family, the house, trees, garage, driveway, the neighbor's houses and yards, by faith, with the Blood of Jesus.

I prayed for the attorneys, the D.A., the Judge, the bailiff, the court reporter and everyone that had anything to so with this matter. I prayed good, not evil. I prayed blessings, not curses. I prayed love, not hate.

I forgot to note the time of my arrival at the prayer site, so when I left I didn't know how long I had prayed, or how many times I encircled the house and property. There was not a neighbor in sight.

Later that night my prayer partner called to tell me that it was a zoo at the court house with TV cameras, reporters and curious onlookers. The Judge said that there was too much commotion and continued the hearing to another date.

He said when he arrived home he expected to see the news media, but he came home to peace and quiet. There were no reporters, thank God, His neighbors (four) called him on the phone to tell him they watched a lady friend of his march around his house that morning while he was in court. (How did they know I was his friend?)

While he was on the telephone talking to me, two men parked down the street from his house (his son was watching) and tried to take pictures of his house from afar. One man had a camera, and one man had a microphone. The camera seemed not to work because the man with it returned to the car three times as if to replace things on it. The other man seemed not to get his microphone to work because he kept hitting it in the palm of his hand.

When the camera and microphone wouldn't work, they left those items in their car and walked toward the house where they would attempt to get an interview or a statement about all that was going on. About half the distance between the house and their car they stopped. They walked slowly until they reached the house. They knocked on the door, his son answered, they asked for a statement, they were told no, they said alright, they turned around and walked to their car, got in their car and drove away. No one approached his house since concerning this matter.

HALLELUJAH, HALLELUJAH, HALLELUJAH, HALLELUJAH.

THANKS TO GOD

Father, I give you thanks and praise. I told my partner what I had done around his house, his property, his family and his neighbors. How by faith, I was led to plead the precious Blood of Jesus on the whole matter. How I believed by faith that: (1) God had encamped angels all around the area: (2)

God had swept the area clean of demonic influences: (3) The strongholds have been pulled and shaken down:

(4) A fortress has been erected around his family and his property. I also shared with my friend (I can now call him my friend because we have been to battle and war together) that this is a matter that he must go through. That he is ordained to go through to the end, and that the favor of God will carry him. This matter is for more that just him and his family. There are others whose hearts may be pricked, and/or others will benefit from the outcome of the matter. Because of his faith in God, in spite of what is happening to him, someone will be saved. We continue to pray and give thanks for protection, enlightenment, guidance, strength and endurance. The situation is about the glory of God and all who God desires to touch. My friend will know that God is in control, because he will be endowed with peace, and a calmness that can't be explained.

Jesus we love you, and we give you glory, honor and all praise. Thank you for your presence.

GALATIANS 6:2

PRAYER FOR SALVATION

My prayer specifically for you is that you have already asked and accepted Jesus Christ into your heart. Whether you have, and especially if you have not, please pray this prayer.

Dear Heavenly Father,

I come to you in the name of Jesus. You said in your Word, *1 John 1:9, If we confess our sins, he is faithful and just to forgive us our sins, and to cleanse us from all unrighteousness.* I ask you to forgive me my sins and cleanse me from all unrighteousness. Thank you for forgiving me.

Romans 10:9, That if thou shalt confess with thy mouth the Lord Jesus, and shall believe in thine heart that God raised him from the dead, thou shalt be saved.

I confess with my mouth that Jesus Christ is the Son of God, and I believe in my heart that God raised him from the dead for my salvation and my justification.

Your Word also says in ***John 6:37, All that the Father giveth me shall come to me; and him that cometh to me I will in no wise cast out.***

By your Word I know that you will take me in and not cast me out, and I thank you for that.

Romans 10:10, For with the heart man believeth unto righteousness; and with the mouth confession is made unto salvation.

Jesus, I ask you to come into my life and save me now. I receive you into my life, and I thank you for your sacrifice and for saving me.

Now that you have accepted Jesus into your life, share your life saving experience with someone, and I pray that you look and find a Bible teaching church where you can be discipled.

Jesus told Nicodemus, ***John 3:5, Verily, Verily, I say unto thee, Except a man be born of water and of the Spirit, he cannot enter into the kingdom of God.***

I pray that as you are led by the Holy Spirit, you will be water baptized.

www.ingramcontent.com/pod-product-compliance
Ingram Content Group UK Ltd.
Pitfield, Milton Keynes, MK11 3LW, UK
UKHW041949230426
12048UKWH00008B/225